Ian Jack has edited *Granta* since 1995. He began his career in journalism on a weekly newspaper in Scotland in the 1960s. Between 1970 and 1986 he worked for the *Sunday Times* as a reporter, editor, feature writer and foreign correspondent (mainly in the Indian Subcontinent). He was a co-founder of the *Independent on Sunday* in 1989 and edited that newspaper between 1991 and 1995. His awards in Britain include those for reporter, journalist and editor of the year. A book of his writing about Britain, *Before the Oil Ran Out*, was published by Secker and Warburg in 1987 and republished by Vintage in 1997. He lives with his family in London.

THE CRASH
THAT
STOPPED BRITAIN

Ian Jack

Granta Books
London

Granta Publications, 2/3 Hanover Yard, London N1 8BE

First published in Great Britain by Granta Books 2001

A CIP catalogue record for this book is available from the
British Library.

1 3 5 7 9 10 8 6 4 2

Typeset by *Granta* magazine

Printed and bound in Great Britain by
Mackays of Chatham PLC

When he worked long ago at the *Sunday Times*, the Australian journalist Murray Sayle used to remark that a good newspaper story can be of two kinds. One, arrow points to defective part. Two, we name the guilty men. The first has always been easier than the second.

1. Howe Dell

About sixteen miles north of central London, just before the town of Hatfield, Hertfordshire, there is a small wooded valley with a stream and a pond at the bottom: Howe Dell. This is an ancient place. Flints attributed to the Mesolithic Age have been found at the stream's bottom. Before the English Reformation the church owned the land—it was the Hatfield Rectory's glebe land—until Henry VIII, who was between third and fourth wives at the time, 'conveyed' it along with the Manor of Hatfield to his growing list of property in 1538. Later in the sixteenth century, it was also at Hatfield, at Hatfield House, that Elizabeth Tudor received the news that she was to be queen.

This information can be read on a sign in the dell, which now has the status of 'a valuable urban wildlife site', houses having been built around three sides of it as Hatfield grew from a village to one of London's outer suburbs. Hornbeam, ash, oak and willow grow in the valley; also carpets of bluebells and dog's mercury—though of course no flowers were visible when I went there last December, nor any of the wrens, chaffinches or blue tits which the sign says haunt Howe Dell. It was a grey afternoon; bare trees, earth sodden from the wettest English autumn since 1727, the year that the keeping of records began. Men from the local housing estates walked their dogs through clinging mud. Electric trains passed close by with their windows lit—dinky little reading lights in the first-class carriages of the expresses—but they travelled slowly.

The railway forms the fourth side of Howe Dell, its eastern and most definite boundary, with a high steel fence to keep out people who might damage the railway or get themselves killed. The tracks of the main line from London King's Cross to the north of England and to Scotland curve here, perhaps because the engineers who surveyed the route in the late 1840s wanted to avoid the cost of embankments and bridges over Howe Dell, or because the landowner was stubborn, or because the Great Northern Railway wanted Hatfield's station to be located in the village rather than an inconvenient mile outside it. Whatever the cause, the four tracks coming down from London bend to the right and east—a gentle enough curve which trains had safely negotiated for 150 years, until October 17, 2000.

On that day at 12.23 p.m. the 12.10 King's Cross to Leeds express entered the curve at 115 miles an hour—the maximum permitted speed for this stretch of track—and came off the rails. Four people died. They were:

Robert Alcorn, aged thirty-seven, a pilot from New Zealand who had been living in London and was travelling to Leeds to fly a Learjet from there to Jersey;

Steve Arthur, aged forty-six and Alcorn's employer as the owner of the Atlantic Gulf Aviation Company, married with two children aged eight and four, of Pease Pottage, West Sussex;

Leslie Gray, aged forty-three, a solicitor, of Tuxford, Nottinghamshire;

Peter Monkhouse, aged fifty, managing director of an advertising company and returning from a meeting in London, married with three children aged twenty-six, twenty-three and fifteen, of Headingley, Leeds.

All four men had been in the buffet car (coach G). Its roof was ripped off when it struck one of the steel stanchions placed regularly at the side of the track to support the line's overhead electric wires. Another seven coaches were derailed; the locomotive and the first two coaches remained on the track. If the same number of dead had been recorded in a motorway accident, it would have been a small news item. It threatened no record in

9

recent British railway crashes (Southall, 1997, seven dead; Ladbroke Grove, 1999, thirty-one dead). Historical comparison made it almost a minor incident (the three-train Quintinshill collision, 1915, 227 dead). But no other railway accident in British history—or, I would guess, any other country's history—has led to the degree of public anger, managerial panic, political confusion, blame and counter-blame that came in the wake of the Hatfield crash. In fact, outside wars and nuclear accidents, it is hard to think of any technological failure which has had such lasting and widespread effects (to those not directly involved, those not struggling for life in the Atlantic or bereaved on land, the *Titanic* was simply a very thrilling story, a chilling entertainment; *Challenger* halted only a space programme). A week or so later, when overfilled rivers began to flood low-lying England and the first people were emptied from their sandbagged homes into boats, the unsettling impression grew of Britain as an unsound country, weakly equipped, under-skilled, easily made chaotic and only superficially modern; an incompetent society. 'We must be the laughing stock of Europe,' people said (and might have been correct). The reason was elementary: movement. People could not move, in an economy—the world's fourth or fifth largest—which depended on millions of everyday, necessary journeys. Few trains ran; those that did ran unreliably, even to the revised schedules that sometimes doubled or trebled the normal journey times. Travellers tried other methods; motorways became impassable, domestic flights overbooked. At railway stations, even aboard a train itself, would-be passengers were advised to travel 'only if your journey is really necessary'; the train may depart, but it may not arrive—nothing could be guaranteed. In any case, what was necessity, how were we to rank it? Arriving at the office? Reaching a funeral? Getting home? The question hadn't been asked in Britain since the belt-tightening poster campaigns (*Is Your Journey Really Necessary?*) of the Second World War. People old enough to remember the Second World War, its long trains packed with troops crawling through blackouts and air raids, compared that period favourably with the present. There was an enemy then; Britain was a more capable nation.

Two months after the crash, as I walked around Howe Dell, none of this had abated. Every day the newspapers reported a new crisis of trust and confidence in the railways and the businesses which own them (NEW RAIL HORROR: MY JOURNEY

TO HELL). I expected to find cut flowers at the site—the 'floral tributes' which mark the place of death by accident or murder on many British streets; bouquets tied to lamp posts and the flashing beacons at pedestrian crossings (there were 3,423 deaths on British roads and thirty-three on railways in 1999). I wanted, I suppose, some bitter monument, the names of the dead attached to a slogan—*Killed by Stubborn Political Ideology*, maybe, or *They Died in the Cause of Profit*; something to set against the sweetness of the wild-flower information of the sign across the stream in the woods. But other than the mud churned up by the cranes and lorries which lifted the wreckage and took it away, there was no evidence that anything fatal and important had ever happened here.

What was the cause of this crash and these deaths? On the night of October 17, various theories were aired—a terrorist bomb, vandalism, some fault with the train, driver error, signal error. By the next day, however, the immediate cause was identified and publicized: a broken rail. A 100ft length of steel became the assassin, the Gavrilo Princip in the case, but, like the sluggish underlying causes and abrupt consequences of the First World War, how and why it came to break and why its shattering dislocated the life of Britain—these causes stretch back and out into the wider world of politics and history beyond Howe Dell.

We could begin in Babylonia.

2. The Permanent Way

When I was five or six years old, my elder brother took me for a walk one day down the hill through the cotton factories—this was Lancashire—to the place where a railway broke free of its tunnel. We scrambled down the embankment. My brother placed a penny on the line. Soon enough a train came past. Afterwards, smoke and steam hung lazily in the tunnel mouth. As the throb of the train receded into the distance, we stepped forward again and retrieved a wider, thinner penny with the head of King George VI flattened and disfigured by the pressure of many tons. (This may have been an offence against the realm as well as the trespass laws; it certainly caused a row when we got home.) That was the first time that I can remember coming close to a rail, bending over its burnished top surface and rusty sides as my brother (who was in the grip of the railway hobby) explained some technical terms: the wooden 'sleepers'—or 'ties' in North America—which hold the two lines of rail

15

together (that day I remember their smell of pitch and creosote); the 'fishplates' which bolt the joins in place between each length of rail and the next; the iron 'chairs' which grip the rail and are bolted to each sleeper; last the 'ballast', the heaped chips of rock into which the sleepers are bedded.

An apparently simple technology, and until the Hatfield crash I never thought about it. Who would? A steel rail to support and guide a powered wheel, a flange on the wheel to keep the wheel in place; result, traction. Writers and painters have been taken by the sheen of rails, their resolute straightness and smooth curves, since they became features of almost every landscape in the nineteenth century: rails by moonlight and in the morning sun, 'shining ribbons of steel', 'the romance of the Iron Road'. In film, they may make their most famous appearance in John Ford's *The Iron Horse*, when the labouring teams which are building America's first transcontinental railway from each coast meet in Utah and hammer the last spike home. In literature, the Australian writer Murray Bail has a fine description in his novel, *Eucalyptus*:

The heavy rails went away parallel to the platform on the regularly spaced sleepers darkened by shadow and grease, and darkened further as they went away into the sunlight, the rails converging with a silver wobble in bushes, bend and mid-morning haze.

How rails look (Bail); how they could unify a nation (Ford); but how did they come to be? The whole assemblage—rails, sleepers, ballast—is known as 'the permanent way', so called to differentiate it from the temporary track which was laid to build the railway, its great earthworks, bridges and tunnels. The permanent way was first perfected in England, and in England still there is a learned and professional society, The Permanent Way Institution, founded by a group of railwaymen in Nottingham in 1884 to 'advance track knowledge and the spreading and exchanging of such knowledge among railwaymen throughout all railway systems at home and abroad'. Today it has 7,000 members—men mainly, though women were admitted in 1964—many of them in former colonies of the British Empire or in other parts of the world such as South America which once imported British railway technology. The institution publishes books and monographs. One of the latter, *The Evolution of Permanent Way* by Charles E.

Lee, first published in 1937 and still distributed to members, addresses the question of history— originally, one suspects, to inspire the institution's membership of permanent way inspectors with an idea of vocation, of historical mission, in their long, often lonely, days and nights spent walking along miles of track. (My own father, a steam mechanic, an artisan, kept a commonplace book which contains, among the poems and pressed flowers, assorted references to George Stephenson and James Watt, so this idea of technological mission, of informing working men of their heroic antecedents, is believable to me.)

And so: Babylonia. According to Lee, a railway 'is merely a specialized form of road designed to meet limited needs'. According to Lee again, the earliest evidence of railways by this definition occurs in the Babylonian empire ruled by Belus, about 2245 BC. Around this time—not much after Middle Stone Age families were sitting around Howe Dell, chipping flints—Babylonian stonemasons were instructed to build certain imperial roads as two parallel lines of stone, 5ft (or three cubits) apart, this distance measured from the centre of each stone line, so that vehicles of the same 5ft axle-width could be pulled along by mules and horses which walked down the centre of the track. This system made haulage easier, the wheels turning against smooth stone rather than rough ground, but it seems (Lee's evidence is sketchy) to have contained no means of making sure that a vehicle stayed on the track other than by the navigational instincts of its animal pullers and human drivers. Railways by their more exact definition, as prepared tracks which by their construction keep the vehicle in place and guide it independently of human or animal interference, were probably first known in Greece. When Aristophanes was alive, around 400 BC, Greek ships were pulled across the isthmus at Corinth on wheeled cradles which travelled along grooves cut into the rock. Elsewhere in Greece, images of the gods were moved to their sacrificial sites along tracks of grooved stone laid to a uniform gauge of 5ft 4in, with loops—*ektropoi*—so that vehicles might pass each other. Regular and parallel grooves, all 4ft 6in apart, can also be found in the streets of Pompeii, though whether they were ruts worn by chariot wheels or a form of guide-rails cut intentionally, Lee cannot be sure.

A prolonged and rail-less interval followed the collapse of Greek and Roman civilizations, until, around the twelfth century, German miners began to spread across central Europe in the search for exploitable seams of metal ore: iron, lead, silver, copper and gold. Illustrated books published in Germany in the sixteenth century have lively woodcuts of bearded men in pointed woollen headwear pushing small trucks from the mine's mouth on wooden rails, while other men, similarly bearded and hatted (mines could be high in the mountains and bitterly cold), busy themselves at the rock face with hammers and picks. These illustrations, in the book *De Re Metallica* (1556) and elsewhere, are the first to depict railways—their little trucks, mines and men eventually serving as the prototypes for the industrial hi-ho situation in Disney's *Snow White* (just as the grooves cut across Corinth are the precursor of Brio's toy track). But keeping the trucks on the wooden track—making them obey, as it were, its direction—remained a large problem when both wheel and rail were flat at their point of contact, with nothing to prevent the one leaving the other. Various methods evolved. Trucks were fitted with guide pins or secondary guide wheels which ran along the rail's inner vertical surface like castors; sometimes the rails themselves were modified with U-shaped channels to hold the wheel or an extra length of wood tacked to their outer sides to form an L-shape and give them a vertical, holding edge. It seems that nobody thought of modifying the wheel rather than the rail—perhaps because the trucks needed to be versatile and run also over rough ground—until railways spread from Europe to Britain in the seventeenth century. The breakthrough was the flange, the edge which extends beyond the wheel's running surface and prevents it going astray. The first documented railway in England (Wollaton, near Nottingham, 1603) probably had trucks with flanged wheels. Like almost every railway built in Britain over the next two centuries, the Wollaton line transported coal from a pithead; and as the coal industry grew— 210,000 tons of it dug between 1551 and 1560, 10,295,000 tons between 1781 and 1790—so railways and flanged wheels proliferated. Lines ran from collieries to ports and canals in many parts of the country; when Bonnie Prince Charlie and his Highland troops defeated the Hanoverian army at the battle of Prestonpans in 1745, they faced cannon positioned on a railway embankment built to serve a Lowland coal mine (the image gives a jolt to romantic history). Chiefly, however, railways grew and developed on the banks of the Wear and Tyne, where the huge volumes of coal taken down steep banks to ships docked on those rivers made road transport increasingly impractical. It was here that the railway took on its modern meaning, as locomotives replaced horses as traction, and wooden rails gave way to iron. Continental Europe, when it came to import the technology of flanged wheels and iron rails from Britain in the last quarter of the eighteenth century, knew it as the *voie anglaise* or the *englischer Schienenweg*—the English railway.

And yet, among all this modernity which placed rough and unlikely stretches of Britain at the leading edge of global change, one thing remained unconsidered and immutable: the width between the parallel rails, the gauge. In Babylonia, in Greece, at Pompeii, if not in the narrow tunnels of the European metal mines, it had always measured somewhere between 4ft and just over 5ft. Now, in Northumberland and Durham, so many miles and years from Babylon, it measured roughly the same. The scholarship of Lee and others suggests that this was the most efficient axle width for animal haulage; narrow it, and the load wouldn't use a horse's full pulling power; widen it, and the weight of the vehicle—the deadweight—would increase disproportionately to the load the vehicle carried. On the multiplying colliery railways of north-east

England, trucks began to be exchanged between coal companies with adjacent lines, and it became important to regularize their gauge. By the end of the eighteenth century many of these railways were 4ft 8in. The steam locomotive provided a massive increase in tractive effort over the horse, and the gauge of a steam-powered railway could have been much wider. But, contrary to its name, the Industrial Revolution arrived by increments. The pioneering steam locomotives of the second decade of the nineteenth century were risky and not always successful experiments as horse-replacements; the gauge existed—there it was trailing down from the pit to the river over expensive bridges and piers; the easiest and cheapest thing was for steam locomotives to adopt it. In 1821, George Stephenson was appointed engineer to an ambitious new railway which would connect the north-eastern towns of Stockton and Darlington, the line which became the world's first public railway—not purely a coal owner's transport—when it was opened in 1825 to all kinds of freight from all kinds of businesses. To build the railway, to carry earth to and from its embankments and cuttings, he hired spoil trucks from the line that served a colliery at Hetton, a few miles off in County Durham. The trucks were of 4ft

8in gauge and the temporary civil-engineering line was built to fit them; Stephenson unquestioningly followed the same width for the permanent way, though sometime in the course of laying it he made a small adjustment. Previously, the right angle of the rail fitted neatly into the other right angle where the wheel joined the flange. This was too rigid for the new power and speed of steam locomotives—the constant scraping of iron against iron in this ninety-degree angle damaged both rail and wheel. Stephenson added the idea of *conicity*, curving the junction between flange and wheel and bevelling the corner of the rail to give greater play between them. Minus its sharp angles on each side, the width between the rails became 4ft 8½in.

This awkward result of conservatism, happenstance and artisanship, expressed by the metric system as 1,435mm, became one of the world's most ubiquitous measurements. When emissaries from other industrializing countries—the US, France, Prussia—came to the Stephenson factory in Newcastle, locomotives designed to that precise gauge were what they saw and sometimes purchased. A steam locomotive could still be so unreliably variable in so many ways—the difficulties and dangers of harnessing steam under pressure—

that it may have been a relief to have one constant, gauge, that could be set aside as an untroubling sine qua non. Why worry about the rail width under the boiler, when the boiler itself might blow up? Easier, if you didn't already possess a railway, to let the locomotive determine the gauge. Later the gauge was questioned, principally by Isambard Kingdom Brunel, who built the main line from London to Bristol at 7ft 1/4in—a more stable and smoother railway, with a far greater carrying capacity—and countries and colonies which first built railways after the gauge question became a public debate adopted various widths: wider in Ireland, Russia and India, narrower in some parts of Australia and Africa. But Stephenson's gauge became the standard where it mattered, in countries at the centre and not the periphery of the industrial world in the first half of the nineteenth century, and in these places Brunel lost his cause.

Of the 750,000 route miles of railway which exist in the world today, sixty per cent measure 4ft 8 1/2in from rail to rail. Across and under the Rockies, the Alps, and the Thames and the Hudson, past the cherry slopes of Mount Fujiyama, spreading into webs of freight yards, converging at junctions; shining and exact parallels, the reasons for their particular exactness lost to the mainstream of history. Trains followed this gauge to the battlefields of the American Civil War and the Somme, into the Vatican City, to the tragic little terminus under the gate at Auschwitz. On this gauge, Buster Keaton outwitted the Union army. Across it, many silent heroines were tied. Riding above it, Cary Grant kissed Eva Marie Saint and remarked: 'The train's a little unsteady' (and in their bedroom on the Twentieth Century Limited, Eva Marie Saint replied: 'Who isn't?').

And of course on October 17 last year it was also the gauge that carried the 12.10 north from London, with 170 passengers including four men of middle age named Alcorn, Arthur, Monkhouse and Gray. Five minutes out of King's Cross, somewhere between Finsbury Park and Hornsey if my frequent experience is any guide, an announcement was made from the buffet car. It was open and selling 'traditional and gourmet sandwiches, hot toasties, pastries, and hot and cold drinks'. Seats could be taken for lunch.

The four men rose from their first-class seats and swayed up the train to coach G. Alexandra Palace went by on its green hill. The train accelerated and bore on through the tunnels and stations of the north London suburbs: New Southgate, Oakleigh Park, New Barnet, Potters Bar. The names of the stations became too blurred by speed to read, the tunnels no more than a momentary darkness and a change of noise and pressure that shuddered the carriage windows.

Thirteen miles out: the first countryside—cows, woods, what might still be a farmhouse. A mobile phone or two rang out its simple tune: *Für Elise*, 'British Grenadiers'. The four men were by now sitting before white tablecloths and waiting for lunch. Alcorn sat across from Arthur at one table, Monkhouse and Gray at another over the aisle. Behind the bar, small bottles of Merlot Cabernet jiggled in a glass cabinet. Steam hissed from the tea and coffee machine. Hot bread filled with bubbling cheese pinged in the microwave.

Fourteen miles out, Brookmans Park. A mile and thirty seconds later, Welham Green. Some flat modern factories and warehouses appeared on the left with large and legible signs: SOUNDCRAFT, TESCO, FALCON FOR GAMES, PUZZLES AND PLAYING CARDS, MITSUBISHI. If any of the four men looked out of the window at this point, Mitsubishi would be the last word he ever read.

27

3. The trouble with rails

The first rails to be made completely of metal came out of the Dowlais ironworks in South Wales in 1791. They were cast iron, much more durable than wood but also brittle; they broke. The great quest in the 210-year history of rails since then has been *to find a rail that will not break*—or not at least inside the parameters of the load it is expected to carry within its allotted lifespan. The answer, for a time, was wrought or malleable iron—iron beaten with hammers or pressed through rollers, rather than poured molten into casts to cool and harden. Wrought iron was more fibrous, many of the impurities had been beaten out of it; it had a greater tensile strength. In 1820, John Birkinshaw of the Bedlington Ironworks in Northumberland patented 'An Improvement in the Construction of Malleable Iron Rails...whereby the Expence of Repairs of broken rails [is] saved'. Each of Birkinshaw's rails had been squeezed six times between the cylinders of his rolling mill and emerged at unprecedented lengths of up to 18ft— 'to reduce the shocks or jolts to which the carriages are subject from passing over the joints (very much to the injury of the machinery)'. Stephenson used Birkinshaw rails for the Stockton and Darlington and again later on the world's first passenger railway, the Liverpool and Manchester, where they were laid in 15ft lengths weighing 35lb a yard. They also broke. By 1832, only two years after the railway opened, it was noticed that fragments of iron littered the track. New rails were ordered at steadily increasing weights, first 50lb a yard, then 60lb, then 75lb. By 1839, every one of the line's original rails had been replaced.

Eleven years later, when the Great Northern Railway opened its main line between London and Peterborough via Hatfield, the pattern was repeated. The trains curved past Howe Dell on 18ft lengths of wrought iron rail which weighed 72lb to the yard. They too soon began to chip and fragment under the weight of heavy coal traffic. A few miles south, at Barnet, it was judged that the life of a rail was no more than three and a half years. The Great Northern ordered new wrought iron rails and upped their weight by 10lb a yard. By 1865, the entire line had been re-railed. But the new rails proved only slightly more reliable than the old. Trains ran at increasing frequency, load and speed and the manufacture of good wrought iron depended too much on human skill, which varied from shift to shift and works to works.

Railways began to experiment with steel—a strong, supple iron alloy formed by blasting air through iron during the smelting process to remove the carbon content, the invention patented by Sir Henry Bessemer in 1855. Steel rails were a third more expensive, but trials showed that they lasted four to six times longer than wrought iron. By the 1880s almost every main line in England, including the Great Northern's, had been relaid in steel, but that too had problems. Steel could last for years, shining brightly in the signal lights, apparently perfect, and then suddenly it would snap. Accidents were rare from this cause, but two passengers died at St Neots, thirty-five miles north of Hatfield, when broken steel rails threw a train off the line in 1895. In 1899, members of the Institution of Civil Engineers in London worried about the 'capricious' nature of steel rails and their 'remarkable vagaries'. British engineers studied the new science of metal fatigue, mainly the work of the German metallurgist, August Wohler (an early example of what became a reverse flow of railway know-how, as Britain imported new knowledge and techniques from Europe and the US). Rails became heavier still; on the line past Howe Dell they weighed 100lb a yard by 1914, 109lb by 1950. Their shape changed. In the middle nineteenth century, rails had been made with the head (the top) the same as the foot (the bottom), to give two potential running surfaces, so that after one was worn out the rail could be turned upside down, doubling its life. The idea didn't work—the base-plates left dents in the bottom surface—but the shape was retained for a hundred years. They were known as 'bullheads', and their replacements in the 1950s as 'flatbottoms'—the usual shape in Europe and North America. The noise made by the combination of track and train began to change around the same time. The wheels no longer ran clackety-clack over the joins ('What's the train saying?' our fathers would say. '*Peas-and-beans, peas-and-beans, peas-and-beans*? Or is it *fish-and-chips, fish-and-chips, fish-and-chips*? What's for tea?') British engineers followed European practice and welded the lengths of rail together. The tiny gap between each rail length disappeared. Concrete sleepers replaced wood, and the rails were bolted or spiked directly to them— no intervening 'chairs'—as the US had done from the beginning. In combination, these changes made the rails more durable and saved money on repairs. When trains ran over continuously welded track the cost of their tractive energy was cut by five per cent, by the single act of removing the tiny gap or the infinitesimal difference in position between one rail and the next; the price of peas-and-beans.

Then, in 1967, forty-nine passengers died when a train derailed on unwelded track at Hither Green in south London. The cause was a rail which had fractured at its weakest point, the bolt-holes at the join. Rails thereafter were made to a new specification, with a thicker 'web'—the spine which joins railhead to railfoot—and a new weight of 113lb.

This became the standard British rail, specification BS11–113A. In 1995, as part of regular repair and maintenance work, new rails of this kind were laid at Howe Dell. Like most rails in Britain, they were made by British Steel (now part of an Anglo-Dutch company, Corus) at its plant in Workington, Cumbria. They weren't quite standard. When rails are expected to carry an extra stress, they are especially hardened at the factory by quenching them with water as soon as they leave the rollers, a process called 'mill heat treatment'. These were mill heat treated (MHT) rails; they were to be laid on the curve. And curves bring their own problems.

4. The trouble with curves

Engineering is often easier to depict than to describe. One striking thing about engineers—apart from their disenchantment with the managerial class set above them and the trivialized culture which neglects them—is how often they want to draw things; words not being up to the work of describing the technical reality. During the research for this piece, I was handed several instant drawings. 'Give us a pen,' engineers would say, 'Look, it works like this.'

In a phenomenon known as 'the dynamics of the wheel/rail interface', drawing is especially useful. One day in November I took the train from London to Peterborough—a very slow train which moved gingerly over the crash site—to meet a young engineer, Philip Haigh, who writes for the specialist magazine, *Rail*. 'Give us a pen,' he said at one point, and then: 'Do you have a 5p piece?' He drew round the circumference of the coin to produce a circle with a diameter of about ³/₄in or 2cm. That was the size of the contact area between a wheel and a rail when train and track were in perfect equilibrium. Perfection requires the straightest rail and the truest wheel; but if these ideal conditions were met, Haigh said, then only a ³/₄in strip would wear along the

33

rail top (which is 2¾in wide). In an electric locomotive, 100 tons of vehicle and machinery could be shared among eight wheels and eight of these 5p contact spots. Each 5p would support a weight of 12.5 tons. Given a powerful engine, the friction caused by turning all eight wheels against two rails would easily haul a train of 1,000 tons at 115 miles an hour.

And when the train reaches a curve? 'The contact spot shifts for both wheel and rail,' Haigh said. What happens is this: the wheels are asked to obey a new direction by the rail. That instruction, combined with centrifugal force, pushes the wheel against the rail on the outside of a curve. The shoulder between flange and wheel hits the corner of the rail. At low speed, that hardly matters, the train will scrape round. At high speed, say 125 mph, the train needs some corrective to try to restore its equilibrium. Therefore the track is 'canted'—tilted like the racing track in a velodrome, with the outside rail the higher of the two. But different kinds of train travel at different speeds and would need different levels of cant if their equilibrium was always to be perfect. Engineers reach a compromise: a cant that will work at different speeds, though not perfectly for all of them. The difference between the ideal cant for a high-speed train and the most practical cant for all trains is known as 'cant deficiency'. At high speed, the wheels still shift position and put an extra stress on the higher rail, attacking its inner corner, the corner from which the gauge is measured: the gauge corner.

Rails are made to take pressure from the top. Exposed to this different, sideways pressure from, say sixty fast trains a day, seven days a week, they can begin to crack: gauge corner cracking. Mill heat treatment prevents that. Or does it? The answer seems to be yes and no. It might modify a rail's first inclination to crack, but once a crack has started, a softer rail may be the better option. Softer rails wear faster, perhaps faster than cracks can grow; a crack can be worn away before it has the chance to dive down into the heart of the rail. In Haigh's phrase, a softer rail can be 'self-correcting'. (Metallurgists and engineers debate this. However, the rails which replaced those destroyed in the crash at Howe Dell were not heat-treated, and no heat-treated rails have been laid in Britain since.)

Curves are by no means the only cause of damaged rails. The steel may contain flaws, little voids (*taches ovales*) which are difficult and

THE HATFIELD CRASH

1. The cause: gauge corner cracking

The normal contact area between wheel and rail is on the rail top. When the wheels of trains travelling at high speed hit a curve, sideways thrust creates a different area of contact by pushing the wheel's flange against the rail's inner or 'gauge' corner.
The stress in the steel, repeated hundreds of times a week, can cause tiny cracks.

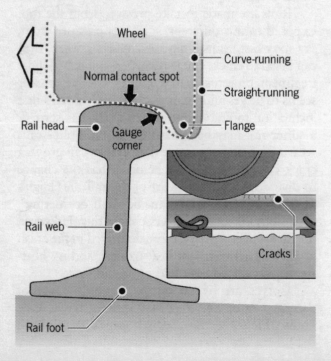

Wheel

Curve-running

Normal contact spot

Straight-running

Rail head

Gauge corner

Flange

Rail web

Cracks

Rail foot

2. The result: derailment at 115mph

On October 17, 2000, the 12.10 London to Leeds express took the curve south of Hatfield at the highest permitted speed. The outer, defective rail on the curve broke at some point after the locomotive and first two coaches passed over it. The rest of the train was derailed. Four passengers died when the buffet car (coach G) hit a steel pole which supports the overhead power line.

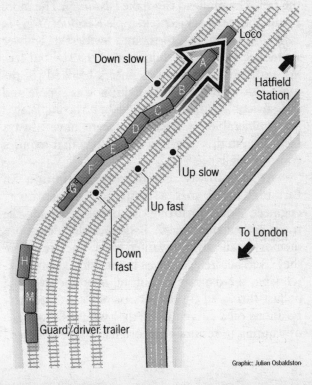

Graphic: Julian Osbaldston

sometimes impossible to detect with the human eye. Wheels which are out of shape and not perfectly circular (*wheel flats*) can batter and dent the rail—like gauge corner cracking, this comes under the general heading of rolling contact fatigue. The ground beneath can subside by an inch and twist the rail. The railhead can flake (*spalling*). The more I read about the subject (example *Residual Stress in Rails*, by Orringer, Orkisz and Swiderski, Kluwer Academic Publishers, volume one, 1992—but let's not go there), the more engineers I talked to, the more I saw rails in a new light; not as simple and indestructible—the Iron Road—but as complicated and vulnerable. Railway engineers have always seen them in this way, as a technology that requires constant vigilance.

At a railway engineering exhibition in Birmingham, I met a retired permanent way engineer, Bill Armstrong, who spoke about the track as 'a living thing'. Ballast could 'develop a memory'; rails always wanted 'to go back to where they lived before'. This was in the context of track-relaying, the dangers of putting new line over old ballast furrowed by sleepers or old rails into new positions on a curve, where they would show signs of wanting to resume their original shape and need to be beaten back, with hammers. Rails were always shifting, settling, creeping this way or that. As the chief permanent way engineer for a large part of Yorkshire, in the old coal district between Doncaster and Leeds, he'd been required to walk every mile of his track twice a year; the main line and three tributary passenger branches, several colliery lines, a large freight yard—many dozens of miles on foot, twice a year, peering at the rails. The inspectors under him walked every mile of track in their care at least once a month; in turn, the sub-inspectors under them walked it at least once a fortnight. Then there were the permanent way gangers—labourers—who would also walk their particular stretch. In this way, every mile of line was patrolled not less than twice a week. Passenger lines were inspected no fewer than three times, usually on Mondays, Wednesdays and Fridays. 'We had a saying,' Armstrong said. 'The uninspected inevitably deteriorates.'

We were talking inside one of the bleak halls of Birmingham's National Exhibition Centre. The Hatfield crash had cast a gloom over this year's trade fair. At a couple of seminars in side rooms I'd heard speakers despair of the national culture: 'a dearth of engineers...a basic lack of engineering competence which is a problem across the board in the industry...not enough people who understand how the infrastructure works or behaves'. In the hall, videos at several stands showed pieces of machinery and stressed that 'safety is our number one priority'. The words had become the new railway mantra.

Armstrong, who was manning a stall for the Permanent Way Institution, said: 'How many folk in this country, even the ones who're interested in railways, know what happens below the wheel? With them, it's always the wheel upwards, the stuff on top, never below the wheel. Below the wheel matters. You know the trouble with England? We've never had the guts to rip things down and start again. It's all make do and mend.' He had an analogy. 'It's like having a wife who keeps asking you to paint the front door when the more important job is to get the damp seen to in the cellar.'

He spoke about an everyday garden nuisance, one apparently far removed from the dynamics of the wheel–rail interface: the weed. 'In the old days you'd never see a weed on the line. That was when you had six chaps working from the same hut, looking after their bit of track. Weeds are unsightly, they're evidence of neglect, they clog the drainage in the ballast, the ballast becomes uneven, the tracks sink or twist. It's like a house, the permanent way. You get your foundations right, you get your drainage right, and you build up from there.'

And now? 'The days of a line being patrolled by a man every day have gone. But it's worse than that. Not only have the maintenance structures disappeared, but the knowledge of what the structures *did* has disappeared.'

The great change happened in the middle years of the 1990s, its centrepiece the Railways Act which was passed by the Conservative government under John Major in 1993. Seven years later, at 12.23 p.m. last October 17, the 12.10 to Leeds came off the tracks. The two events are connected.

There was a fracture on the outer high rail at the Hatfield curve. The locomotive and the train's first two coaches passed over it safely, but the shock and pressure ran through the rail like a lightning bolt. The pressure found other cracks; there were cracks everywhere. Instantly, more than a 100ft of rail shattered into 300 pieces. The other eight vehicles came off the track. Passengers fell over each other, necks hit the backs of seats. Scalding water exploded in the buffet car. Apart from the dead—

Alcorn, Arthur, Monkhouse and Gray—two buffet attendants and two other passengers were seriously injured, another sixty-six passengers slightly so. Inside a length of 600 yards and a time of seventeen seconds, a train travelling at 115 mph had broken apart and shuddered to a halt.

Ambulances came. Howe Dell flickered with flashing lights and the arcing sparks of acetylene torches. By 2.30 p.m., the first officers had arrived from government agencies: the Health and Safety Executive, its quaintly named subdivision Her Majesty's Railway Inspectorate, and the British Transport Police. For the next four days they bent among the ballast and the grass and picked up pieces of steel. Eventually they reconstructed the assassin, the rail, and named the assassin's weapon, gauge corner cracking. A remote technical term entered the common language. But if rail and cracks were Gavrilo Princip and his pistol, who was the Kaiser in the case? The truth is that there were several kaisers—stubborn men in love with a political idea that they imagined would fulfil the national destiny. One of them lived just down the track at Huntingdon: the former prime minister, John Major.

5. Trainspotting

Railways as an interest, a hobby like philately or butterfly collecting, began in the late nineteenth century, when English gentlemen with time on their hands (lawyers, vicars) started to see steam locomotives as fascinating objects in themselves rather than purely as the source of the most convenient means of transport. They would pursue rare types, exchange notes, lug plate cameras and tripods to the tops of cuttings, take photographs of expresses (always from a distance and head on, to avoid too much blurring). By 1897 two magazines catered for these hobbyists. Two years later they had a club, the Railway Club, with armchaired rooms in London.

What would one of these trainspotters have seen at Howe Dell? The Great Northern Railway had been built to shorten the distance from London to Yorkshire, to compete against a longer and slower route, and in the closing decades of the nineteenth century it had a service of swift and regular trains which was said to be unrivalled in the world. In 1889, the Shah of Persia came down the 185 miles from Leeds to London in three hours forty-two minutes, and that included a fifteen-minute stop for lunch at Grantham (where Mrs Margaret, now

Baroness, Thatcher's grandfather was a station cloakroom attendant). An enthusiast leaning on the fence at Howe Dell would have seen smart little green locomotives and teak-brown carriages rushing north at a mile a minute, and long coal trains winding slowly south from the northern coalfields to the London depots. Gleaming paintwork and brass, the oil lamp of a signal flickering red though the smoke: superficially, the golden age of Britain's railways. Less golden, however, to the railway shareholder. Britain had a denser network of railways than any other country; travellers from London to Manchester, for example, could choose between four different routes owned by four different companies. Such extreme competition cut into profits. The average return on railway shares between 1850 and 1875 was a modest 3.65 per cent. The most profitable lines were often small local monopolies whose main business was the transport of minerals. Many companies made no money at all. Public ownership was considered by governments as early as the First World War, but in 1923 a different solution was chosen. Britain's 120 railway companies were amalgamated into four large groups, with the government intending that each of them would become a profitable regional monopoly. The Great Northern became part of the London and

North Eastern Railway, the LNER. It built more powerful locomotives and painted them a lighter green; its expresses to the north got faster; in 1938, it claimed the world record speed for a steam locomotive, 126 mph, which has never been bettered. But profit was still difficult because by now the competition wasn't from rival railway companies but from a new means of transport: roads. In the years leading up to the Second World War, the LNER paid its shareholders no dividends at all. In 1946, it managed 0.41 per cent. For a Labour government committed to the post-war reconstruction of Britain's damaged infrastructure, there could be only one solution. In 1948, as part of a pattern common throughout Europe, the railways of Britain were taken into public ownership and became British Railways, later British Rail.

Initial public investment halted their decline, but that proved temporary. Roads increasingly drew away their freight and passengers, and their subsidy became unpopular in the Treasury. Golden Ageism was never far from the surface of post-war Britain, and the feeling grew, especially among Conservative politicians and commentators, that things had been better arranged in the days of gleaming paintwork and brass, when porters tipped their caps when you slipped them sixpence. Over the next thirty years, the railways were 'rationalized'—lines closed, staff cut—until by the 1980s they were the most cost-effective and had the lowest level of government subsidy of any country in western Europe (still unchanged in 1996, when the figures for planned investment over the following four years, per head of population, were: France, £21; Switzerland, £40; Italy, £33; Britain, £9). There was by this time no political belief in them. Mrs Thatcher, the railwayman's granddaughter, made a point of never travelling by train and spoke of 'the great car economy'. Two other phrases began to be applied to railways in her era: 'value engineering' and 'the management of decline'. In the late 1980s, when the East Coast Main Line through Hatfield was electrified, first to Leeds and than all the way to Edinburgh, it was said to be the cheapest such scheme in Europe, where countries such as France and Italy copied the Japanese model and built, at great expense, new straight railways dedicated to high-speed trains, with their rails embedded in continuous concrete. In France, the permitted top speed was 300 kilometres per hour; in Germany, 280 kph; in Italy, 250 kph; in Britain, 200 kph (125 mph). In Britain, the new trains through Hatfield were built at a cost of 23,100 US dollars per seat. In Europe, nothing similar was achieved for under 35,885 US dollars per seat (the new trains built for the Channel Tunnel, London to Paris, cost almost 50,000 US dollars per seat). In Britain, the overhead power lines would blow down in high winds. Their suspension support was not robust.

Within railways, among railway people, there came an important cultural shift. The future of subsidies was uncertain, 'profit-centres' had been created. In this climate, operators—the executives who timetabled and managed the trains—became more important than engineers. In the words of Michael Casebourne, the chief executive of the Institution of Civil Engineers: 'The railways had a tremendous number of engineers, sometimes leading authorities in rail engineering worldwide or in touch with other people who were. They were authoritarian, highly responsible and very good at what they did, and they ran the railway from a protective point of view. An awful lot of what they did—resignalling and track work—interrupted the running of the trains. Consequently, they got a very bad name with the operators, and just before privatization the balance changed—it became an operators' rather than an engineers' railway.'

Privatization, Casebourne added, 'had the effect of reinforcing many of these views'.

6. Ideology

During successive Conservative governments between 1979 and 1997 more than two thirds of Britain's state-owned industry was sold to the private sector, transferring about a million jobs and raising £65bn for the Treasury. Mrs Thatcher wanted to 'roll back the frontiers of the state'; a wider spread of shareholders would create 'popular capitalism', and by exposing state industries to market forces they would become more efficient and offer cheaper goods or a better service to the consumer. The cash raised meant that the government could avoid the more electorally dangerous alternatives of raising taxes or cutting public expenditure. Harold Macmillan, a former and more patrician Conservative prime minister, called it 'selling the family silver'.

The results were uneven. Several public utilities—the gas, water and telecommunications industries—were sold off en bloc to become private monopolies, no more responsive to the market or the consumer than when they were owned by the state. There was public disenchantment. Advocates of privatization blamed lack of competition, which in their view was the key element in raising efficiency. When the turn came for the electricity industry to be privatized, the government broke it down into more than a dozen generating and distribution companies. This seemed to work; competition between them produced 'efficiency', i.e. lower costs. The promotion of competition became a key element in future privatization schemes, and the electricity industry a model for the railways.

By several accounts, Mrs Thatcher had little personal enthusiasm for privatizing British Rail, realizing (perhaps) that if it went wrong she risked the Conservative vote in the London commuter belt. Unlike the electricity industry, trains—and the fares charged to ride on them—depended on a government subsidy that was running close to £1bn a year. But two of her successive Ministers for Transport, Paul Channon and Cecil Parkinson, eventually persuaded her to include it in the Conservative agenda, and in 1990 Parkinson announced to Parliament that the government was 'determined to privatize British Rail'.

Nobody had any clear idea of how, or at least no single clear idea that had across the board appeal to Conservative think tanks, Cabinet ministers, transport economists, civil servants and British Rail itself. Ideas varied. One obvious solution was to break British Rail into several regional monopolies in a new version of the railway companies which existed between 1923 and 1948. Mrs Thatcher's successor, the English nostalgist John Major, seemed for a time to favour that option, and the Conservative manifesto for the 1992 general election included the hope that the new railways would 'reflect regional and local identity [and] recapture the spirit of the old regional companies'. But the trouble with this scenario of gleaming paint and polite porters—Major himself mentioned the Great Western Railway's brown and cream carriages— was that it introduced very little in the way of a new competitive element (ignoring the fact that competition against rival forms of transport, roads and airlines, already existed). A structure needed to be found which would provide competition within the railway itself—and it needed to be found quickly. Major won the 1992 election with his railway privatization scheme little more than a blank piece of paper (in the later words of his new Transport Minister, John MacGregor); the legislation would need to be passed and the privatization successfully implemented by the time the next election was due in 1997. There was very little else left to privatize, and Major, who was aware of his mild public image, needed a privatization of his own to demonstrate his credentials as Mrs Thatcher's fearless heir.

Horizontal separation—the railways as regional monopolies—kept trains, stations, track, signalling and general infrastructure under one ownership, the way they had always been. Vertical separation was a more radical solution. It would separate trains from rails. The owner of the rails would charge the owners of the trains for access to them, on the same principle as a toll road. Different train owners could compete for passengers and freight on the same stretch of track. The idea found favour in Major's old department, the Treasury, and though the object of it has never been achieved (very few train companies compete for the same traffic over the same line), the competitive principle behind it was used to fragment Britain's railways into more than a hundred separate businesses, about the same number that had been amalgamated in 1923.

When the plan was published in a White Paper in 1992, it aroused considerable hostility. Opinion polls showed that a large majority of the public was against it, the Labour Party in opposition fought it, and even the Conservative press was sceptical. The

Conservative Party itself was divided. A Conservative Member of Parliament, the late Robert Adley, interrogated ministers from his position as the chairman of Parliament's Transport Select Committee, and concluded that 'it seems to me that none of them, quite frankly, have a clue about how all this is going to be worked out'. Of all privatization schemes, the railways soon became the most disliked, with few supporters beyond the government and the financiers and commercial lawyers of the City of London who stood to gain. One Transport Minister succeeded another—a total of six in seven years, each as uncertain as his predecessor—but Major and his government stubbornly pressed ahead with the legislation, and on April 1, 1994, the Railways Act came into effect. British Rail's assets could now be sold off, under a plan that had six broad elements and a flurry of acronyms.

The passenger trains were to be run by twenty-five Train Operating Companies (TOCs) on franchises which ran from between seven and fifteen years.

The trains would be owned by three Rolling Stock Companies (ROSCOs) which would lease them to the TOCs.

The railway signalling, the permanent way, bridges, tunnels and some of the larger stations would be owned by one large infrastructure company, Railtrack.

Railtrack would contract out the maintenance and renewal of the infrastructure by competitive tender to civil engineering companies (which had bought British Rail's engineering assets). They in turn might put out the work to subcontractors.

A new independent body, the Office of the Rail Regulator (ORR), would set the amount that Railtrack was allowed to charge the TOCs—the track access charges—and in general promote competition, efficiency and safety inside Railtrack, to the eventual benefit of passengers.

Another new body, the Office of Passenger Rail Franchising (OPRAF) would decide which TOC got which franchise, adjudicate the level of public subsidy required by the TOC (this was a privatization that actually increased public subsidy rather than ending or shrinking it), and reward or penalize train operating performance through a system of bonuses and penalties. Later, under the Labour Government, OPRAF became the Strategic Rail Authority, the SRA.

Six years later, it was hard to find anyone who

would defend this structure, outside the Labour Government. A paradox. In opposition the Labour Party was committed to dismantling privatization and restoring a 'publicly-owned, publicly-accountable railway'. On March 23, 1995, the party's new leader, Tony Blair, described the privatization plan as 'absurd'. He said: 'They [the Conservatives] want to replace a comprehensive, coordinated national railway network with a hotchpotch of private companies linked together by a gigantic bureaucratic paperchase of contracts—overseen of course by a clutch of quangos [quasi-autonomous non-governmental organizations, then a favourite opposition target]. As the public learn more about the chaos and cost, their anger at this folly will grow.' The prediction came true in every respect. But as the 1997 election came closer, the party changed its stance. Under the influence of Gordon Brown, later the head of the Treasury as Chancellor of the Exchequer, no such commitment was included in the manifesto. Labour was anxious to be seen as 'prudent'; taking back the railways, or even just Railtrack, into public ownership would cost too much. In any case, as Brown told a colleague, 'privatization will make the Tories unpopular and save us from having to do it'. In government, Prime Minister Blair told an early Cabinet meeting that railways were 'not a priority'.

British Rail was sold for a total of £5bn. Government subsidies to the railway industry for the three years 1997–2000 come to roughly the same amount. Railtrack, which owned the infrastructure, was sold for £1.93bn in a public flotation. Its market value by 2000 was just under three times as much. Thanks to stubborn political pressure, emanating from a prime minister who feared to be seen as weak, the railways had been sold off hastily, cheaply and carelessly, often to owners for whom 'the wheel/rail interface' was a term of management rather than science (if it meant anything to them at all). Of Railtrack's fourteen board members, only two had railway experience. From 1997 they were led by a chief executive, Gerald Corbett, who had previously worked as the finance director for the hotels and leisure group, Grand Metropolitan. Corbett, who bears a striking resemblance to the English character actor Timothy West, became a familiar figure on television after the crash at Ladbroke Grove in 1999 and again after Hatfield. He was sincere and he was sorry, so much so that, after Hatfield, Railtrack adopted a new slogan, SORRY IS NOT ENOUGH, and pasted it to the windows of its London headquarters and on poster sites by the side of the track. No irony seemed intended personally against the chief executive; the poster went on to say that Railtrack was working hard to give Britain a first-class railway system. At Victoria station, some delayed passenger had seen a nice anagram. The graffiti on the poster read LIARTRACK.

In other ways Corbett's regime at Railtrack could be seen as a success. The company made a profit, its share price rose steeply and the shares paid growing dividends (26.9p per share for the financial year 1999–2000, increased by five per cent after the Hatfield crash to keep the confidence of shareholders). Property was one source of profit. In the four years since Railtrack's flotation in 1996, the rent and sale of some of the buildings and land which the company had so cheaply acquired raised more than £500m. In 1999–2000, about a quarter of total profit came from property sales alone. Railtrack's chief income, however, came from the track access charges paid by the train operators— charges which were fixed in the public interest at retail price inflation minus two per cent by the Rail Regulator. If the train operators ran more trains, the charges could be adjusted upwards, but very slightly; in 1995 nobody, including the Rail Regulator, expected more trains. Five years later, the figure for passenger mileage had grown by thirty per cent and for freight by forty per cent as Britain came out of economic recession, motorways got clogged and train operators adopted aggressive marketing. More people were using the railways than at any time since 1946. The rails they used took more wear, but only a fraction of the increased revenue from passengers was passed on to Railtrack. Worse, more trains meant more track congestion and more delays. The Rail Regulator had set targets for punctuality expressed in percentage points. Every percentage point missed and judged to be Railtrack's fault led to a fine of £1m. In 2000, Railtrack faced a fine of £10m.

So how to make a profit from the infrastructure itself, or at least keep the cost of maintaining it down? The answer lay in scrutinizing the fine print of contractual obligation and putting more work out to tender, 'efficiency savings' which the Rail Regulator himself was keen on. In the aftermath of three rail disasters, this was said to be 'putting profit before safety'. On the trackside, it was rarely as simple as that.

At Hatfield, the technology of track and trains

was now split among at least five different managements. Two companies ran the passenger trains: West Anglia Great Northern (WAGN) to the suburbs and Cambridge; the Great North Eastern Railway (GNER) to Leeds, Newcastle and Scotland, with trains leased from a separate rolling-stock company. Railtrack ran the signalling and owned the line. The line was maintained and repaired by the civil engineers, Balfour Beatty, under contract to Railtrack. Another civil engineering firm, Jarvis, had the contract for track replacement.

The 12.10 GNER express to Leeds was ultimately owned by a bank (the Hong Kong and Shanghai), leased by a Bermuda-registered shipping company (GNER is a subsidiary of Sea Containers), and given its green light by a Railtrack signaller. None of them was at fault. The trouble was the rail.

7. Workers

My route to work in London every morning takes me over a railway bridge. A traveller on the top deck of a bus at this point can see a junction and a single line curving off into a tunnel. Once there were two lines; once the curve was smooth. Sometime in the early 1990s, however, I noticed that one of the lines had been taken up and that the curve was really a series of angled straight rails. Bill Armstrong, the former permanent way man, described this to me as 'a threepenny-bit curve', after the old British twelve-sided coin. The rails had probably been used elsewhere, or turned around at the same site, and wanted to assume their previous form, 'to go back,' as he said, 'to where they lived before'. Also, around the same time, I began to notice weeds here and on other lines; weeds that grew on the ballast sometimes to the size of small shrubs. Even the busy track outside Waterloo terminus had them, with their suggestion of abandoned railways in the Argentinian pampas. I imagined that railways were obeying a new ecological stricture to ban herbicide. The cause was more straightforward.

Between 1992 and 1997, the number of people employed on Britain's railways fell from 159,000 to 92,000 at a time when the number of trains increased. Within these totals, the numbers of workers permanently employed to maintain and renew the infrastructure fell from 31,000 to between 15,000 and 19,000. In a rare piece of enquiring journalism on the subject, the *Guardian*'s labour correspondent, Keith Harper, interviewed some permanent way workers in March, 1998.

They were men aged between forty-five and fifty, 'the rump of what is left of British Rail's skilled workforce,' as Harper described them, and they spoke scathingly of the methods of their new employers, the private contractors who worked for Railtrack. Harper kept them anonymous; speaking to the press—'whistle-blowing'—is now usually a breach of contract. One worker said:

> At least fifty per cent of the track is on its last legs. If it's not broken rails, it's broken components. If the public knew the full picture, it would be horrified. There are accidents waiting to happen and loads of speed restrictions. Some cowboy [casual worker] the other day forgot to put up a 20 mph speed restriction on a 70 mph route. How there wasn't an accident I'll never know.

Another said:

> Railtrack is really responsible for seeing that the work gets done properly, but my work has never been checked by Railtrack and, in my time, I have worked on some extremely dodgy jobs that require proper inspection. It is up to the

maintenance companies to do it, but they often sub-contract work to many fly-by-night operators. They bring in gangs of casuals in taxis and pay them eighty pounds in hard cash for a shift.

A third said:

Railtrack is a joke. It is totally reliant on the maintenance companies and does not know what is going on. Railtrack is so pious. It wrings its hands and says that safety is paramount, yet it gets really nasty if we cannot do a job on time, usually because the time we get to do it is impossible.

In November last year, attending a session of the government inquiry into the Ladbroke Grove rail crash (October 5, 1999, thirty-one dead) before Lord Cullen, I heard the same situation on the track described in a more academic way. Professor Christopher Baldry, head of the Department of Management and Organization at Stirling University, was giving evidence about safety practices among permanent way workers, based on recent research. He used the phrase 'work intensification'.

Counsel: 'What is that?'

Baldry: 'Well, work intensification...can either be the same number of people producing more over a given time period, the same number of people producing the same volume over a shorter time period or a smaller number of people producing a given volume, if technology and other factors are held constant.'

Counsel: 'When you look at the work intensification and the figures which support that, the conclusion which you reach is that there is a worsening safety record and a worsening trend in employee safety in the [railway] industry?'

Baldry: 'Yes, this seemed to us [himself and his fellow researcher] to be what was indicated by the figures. Basically we took the figures for the amount of traffic in rail miles, an index of workload, we looked at the decline in direct employees of both Railtrack and the major contractors, although...this does not include subcontractors which is one of the defects of the official figures, but certainly the continuing downward trend in employment and the continuing upward trend in the amount of traffic carried, I think you can take as an index of work intensification: a smaller number of people are coping with a larger volume of traffic in the network.'

How had this happened? Baldry:

If you are bidding for a contract on what is essentially a labour-intensive process, the only way or one of the major ways you are more likely to win the contract is through offering to do it with reduced labour costs, that is either to do the work with a smaller number of people or in a shorter timeframe.

Baldry went on to describe the long and unregulated hours that could be worked under the negligent eye of a subcontractor, the lack of communication between train crews, signallers and permanent way men—now all employed by different companies and often new to their jobs—and the rivalry between different contractors or subcontractors.

We were given on several occasions evidence that if, for example, track workers from Scotland had been sent down to York to work on a bit of track that was unfamiliar to them, they find themselves working with other employees of a different contractor. Their instinct is to ask local people about the nature of the track. The local people may have been told by their employer 'Don't talk to these persons because they are employed by the opposition.' In other words, there are actual obstacles put in the way of site knowledge and hazards knowledge. We encountered that in several locations.

Familiarity with the track had gone, old patterns of trust had been broken; the price of the competitive spirit. There could be so many different companies employed on the same stretch of line, Baldry said, that it would take 'a very brave person' to halt the work because of a potential hazard. He had heard reports that safety representatives had been threatened with physical violence when they suggested that work should stop. 'It takes quite a brave individual to say stop the work, because of the financial penalties that then rebound back up the system if the work in progress runs over time.' The system that Baldry mentioned was designed by commercial lawyers, in the legal belief that punishment works, and it involves confusing flows of money and paperwork through many 'interfaces'—here the term is managerial rather than scientific—between groups which have different and sometimes conflicting financial interests. When a contracting firm repairs a track, it 'takes possession' of it. Trains are stopped for the duration of these 'track possessions', and this may in itself cost Railtrack money if it cannot meet its obligations to the train operating companies, and their trains are cancelled or delayed. If a track possession overruns its scheduled time, however, the penalties are fiercer. Track work usually takes place at the weekend—but say something unexpected occurs, or the contractor has underestimated the time the repairs will take, and the track possession runs into Monday morning? There is a schedule with tariffs. Rates differ. A delay to a train in the London morning rush hour, for example, can cost Railtrack £200 a minute at Waterloo and £147 a minute at Euston. One delayed train can cause other delayed trains for hundreds of miles down the track, with Railtrack compensating their operators for each. A bill of £250,000 is quite easy to run up. Railtrack, therefore, can penalize the contractor, gathering in money with one hand as it pays out with the other. Whatever emotion this system appeals to—fear, greed, blame, retribution—it is unlikely to inspire either trust or careful workmanship. (Imagine the following sequence of events. A man working for a contractor on the line notices that a rail has some cracks. He consults his supervisor. His supervisor consults Railtrack. How long will the rail last? A track possession will delay trains and cost money. Can a repair be done quickly? Might it be postponed? Need it be done at all? Doesn't it suit the contractor to have the rail replaced at Railtrack's cost, via another contractor? A new rail will cost the maintenance contractor less to maintain. That, a suspicious Railtrack official might think, might lead the contractor to overestimate the damage. Which person, at what rank, will decide what must be done?)

In July 1999, the government appointed a new Rail Regulator, Tom Winsor, a commercial lawyer. Winsor was determined to be tough. He wanted the trains to run to time. For him, Railtrack was 'a supplier not a dictator…it is not the king, that position belongs to the customer'. There was 'no inherent conflict between growth and performance and safety'. Still, safety began to worry both him and railway inspectors at the Health and Safety Executive. A month after Winsor became Rail

Regulator, a Health and Safety report (the Railway Safety Statistics Bulletin 1998–99) showed an alarming increase in the number of broken rails, up by twenty-one per cent on the previous year—937 actual breakages against a Railtrack forecast of 600. On the same day, August 12, he wrote to Gerald Corbett at Railtrack demanding an 'action plan'. A fierce correspondence followed throughout the rest of the year and into 2000. Winsor accused Railtrack of lacking 'effective asset management'. When, on September 1, 1999, Railtrack explained that the increase in broken rails was caused partly by 'rail nearing the end of its life in high tonnage routes', Winsor replied that the spate of rail breaks 'does not seem to suggest that the rail was *nearing* life expiry, but that it was already *at*, or even *beyond* life expiry' [his italics]. Winsor's letters demanded details of likely causes and proposed remedies and suggested that the number of broken rails was prima facie evidence that Railtrack was breaching its government licence to run the infrastructure. In July 2000, Railtrack 'categorically refuted' the allegation that the backlog of track defects had built up because resources were being diverted elsewhere. Winsor and the Health and Safety Executive then looked abroad for expert and independent advice and commissioned an investigation from the Transportation Technology Center in Colorado into Railtrack's method of managing broken rails. The Center produced an extensive and highly critical report which attributed the breakages to a falling rate of rail renewals in the 1990s and a later increase in traffic, and recommended that Railtrack and its contractors should inspect and replace rails more often.

The report was published eight days after the Hatfield crash. When the American researchers completed their work, nobody had died because of a broken rail since 1967. But at the curve, sixteen miles up the line from the bureaucratic anger in London, the rail had continued to crack as the letters went back and forth between Winsor and Corbett. Hour after hour, day after day, expresses rode over it at 115 mph.

8. Blame

Many people knew about this cracking rail. In November 1999, four years after it had been laid, workers for Balfour Beatty, the maintenance contractor, noticed early evidence of gauge corner cracking. Their superiors knew the rail would have to be replaced eventually—the question was when.

Tiny cracks may grow quickly or slowly or might not grow at all—aircraft engineers inspecting aircraft frames make similar calculations. Balfour Beatty suggested to Railtrack that 'rail-grinding' might be a temporary remedy, wearing down the surface of the rail by machine so that the cracks were ground-out before they could grow. Rail-grinding, however, had been suspended soon after the railways were privatized. There was only one operational machine in the country. Nothing came of the idea at the time. Then, at a site meeting between Balfour Beatty and Railtrack in February 2000, a decision was made to replace the rail and Balfour Beatty was invited to bid for the job. Soon after, however, Railtrack informed Balfour Beatty that the work would go instead to Jarvis, the company which had the contract for track renewal as opposed to track maintenance (the boundary between renewal and maintenance can be unclear). A twenty-seven hour 'track possession' was scheduled for March 19. But when that date came, the replacement rail had not arrived at the site. According to John Ware, who investigated the crash for a BBC *Panorama* programme, there had been 'a cock-up in delivery' which might have stemmed in part from the confusing management of the freight wagon carrying the new rails; it was owned by

Railtrack but operated by men from Jarvis. Eventually, towards the end of April, the new rails were successfully delivered and lay by the trackside. A new problem arose: in March, Railtrack and Jarvis had a track-possession slot but no new rails, now they had rails but no new track-possession slot. Could one be arranged in May? The new and busier summer timetable of trains began in that month; closing a stretch of line would cause more inconvenience and delay than in March, and incur penalty payments on Railtrack. Jarvis (again according to John Ware) said it would need five eight-hour possessions. Railtrack countered with the offer of two possessions each lasting four hours and twenty minutes. Jarvis said that to do the work in that time would be physically impossible. The re-railing was postponed until November, when Railtrack were again prepared to offer eight-hour possessions during the less crowded winter timetable. In September, a grinding-machine finally came and wore down the rail's surface, which might have been the wrong treatment at the wrong time. Grinding is meant to stop cracks growing; if the cracks have already grown beneath the surface, some engineers believe that grinding can make a cracked rail weaker.

In the meantime the rail continued to be inspected by Balfour Beatty, once a week by human eye (a man walking along the track), once every three months ultrasonically by a machine which is pushed by hand along the rail to scan its interior. This, for a high rail on a high-speed curve, was normal practice. The rail was scanned ultrasonically in April and again in July and by Railtrack's admission at least one of these scans was classified as unreadable. An unreadable ultrasonic scan suggests that either the cracking is so extensive that the machine can't register it, or that there is a fault in the machine. In either case, the rules suggest that a 20 mph speed limit should automatically be imposed. Even without ultrasonic scanning, all the available evidence suggests that the Hatfield rail had been, or should have been, recognized as a most dangerous rail which demanded the imposition of a speed limit. When the rail was reassembled, it bore obvious signs of pre-crash metal distress. Apart from the cracking, its top surface had flaked up to a depth of three millimetres. A speed limit would have prevented four deaths.

On the day after the crash, Railtrack admitted that the condition of the rail was 'wholly unacceptable'. Later, before the House of Commons

Select Committee on Transport, Gerald Corbett went further and said the rail was in an 'appalling' state. He couldn't understand why a speed limit hadn't been imposed: it was 'either incompetence or a systems failure, or...there might be a cultural aspect to it'. Tom Winsor, the Rail Regulator, concluded that there had been 'almost certainly a failure in the chain of command...between Railtrack and the organization engaged to carry out maintenance on that piece of network'. The Commons committee concluded that it was 'clear that Railtrack's management of Balfour Beatty...prior to October 17 was totally inadequate'.

How much did Balfour Beatty and Jarvis tell Railtrack? What were Railtrack's instructions to Balfour Beatty? Which people are at fault? Who are the guilty men? As I write, in early March, police investigations continue. Witnesses have been reluctant to be interviewed. There are filing cabinets of documents to be read. The evidence may support a criminal prosecution. The public mood, so far as one can tell, would like big fish in the net and a charge of corporate manslaughter. That is unlikely; as someone close to the Hatfield investigation said to me, you would need to find a piece of paper with such improbable words written on it as *Do not repair this track, we can't afford it. Yrs sincerely, The Fat Controller*. More likely is a charge of manslaughter—culpable homicide—made against individuals lower down the management ladder, or their prosecution for a breach of the Health and Safety at Work Act.

Corbett offered his resignation to the Railtrack board on October 18 and had it rejected. Railtrack's management was by now in a shaking fuddle. On the night of the crash, Railtrack had imposed emergency speed restrictions at eighty other high-speed curves which had gauge corner cracking, extending this later to any site where it judged the cracking to be 'severe'—that is, with cracks measuring more than 30mm long. Now the Health and Safety Executive wondered about cracks in the next category down Railtrack's scale, those defined as 'heavy' and between 20 and 29mm long. What was the scientific basis for this fine difference? Was 'heavy' cracking not just as potentially dangerous as 'severe'? Railtrack agreed that speed limits, some as low as 5 mph, should be imposed on both categories, and remain in place until the rail had been replaced or ultrasonically tested and cleared. Soon there were speed restrictions at 800 sites, and a 'National Track Recovery Programme' which promised to replace 300 miles of rail and 860 switches and crossings by January. The implication, which Railtrack could never successfully refute, was that millions of passengers had been riding at high speed over lethally-flawed track for several years. Some important lines closed entirely; for a day or two, Glasgow was cut off from the south. The economies of large cities such as Leeds and Newcastle began to suffer. London's department stores and theatres were unusually empty. The Queen abandoned the train for an official visit to Cambridge. The Royal Mail switched its parcels and letters to chartered aircraft. Journey times doubled and trebled. On November 27, Britain's railways established a peacetime record for slowness when passengers on the 10 p.m. express from London to Nottingham reached their destination at 7 a.m. the next day; a journey of 126 miles had taken nine hours. Railtrack promised a normal timetable by Christmas. At Christmas, normality was postponed to Easter. A National Rail Recovery Plan was announced. The Prime Minister called 'rail summits' at which heads would be 'knocked together'. On December 12, he conceded that it was 'absolute hell travelling on the railways' and promised that if the situation was not sorted out by January he would use 'the necessary powers…to issue guidance to speed this whole process up'. That was his biggest stick. The growing demand to have the railway infrastructure taken back into public ownership was firmly rejected, though it had supporters (columnists in *The Times* and *Daily Mail*, for example) who had political positions far removed from the Prime Minister's least favourite word, socialism. Railtrack: who could deny the oddity and scandal of it? It took public money and paid private dividends; it received continual instructions and interference from the government via the Rail Regulator; its revenues were fixed; it couldn't grow; it didn't work. But it was convenient for governments: in one columnist's words, it allowed 'the nationalization of credit and the privatization of blame'.

Its chief executive, Gerald Corbett, was interviewed on BBC Television two days after the crash and the day after he'd offered to resign. He said: 'The railways were ripped apart at privatization and the structure that was put in place was a structure designed, if we are honest, to maximize the proceeds to the Treasury. It was not a structure designed to optimize safety, optimize investment or, indeed, cope with the huge increase in the number of passengers the railway has seen.'

On November 10 he gave evidence to the Cullen Inquiry.

Counsel: 'In statements made to the media you have indicated that, in your view, there are fundamental structural flaws in the privatized industry. You have called for a restructuring of the industry in what has been described as a personal manifesto for fundamental change. Indeed, in your own statement, at page 4, paragraph 11, you yourself quote part of an interview that you gave to BBC *Newsnight* on October 19. On another occasion you announced publicly that we have got to think the unthinkable, that we have got to think radically.

'Mr Corbett, all this appears to suggest that there has been a radical change in your view of the structure of the railway and, given that this change appeared to manifest itself post-Hatfield, that the rail at Hatfield was, if you like, a "Road to Damascus". What I want to explore with you is whether that is correct and the degree to which you consider that the problems currently facing the railways are of a fundamental nature, fundamental structural problems?'

Corbett: 'Yes. I do not believe that I have ever

come up with a personal manifesto and I do not believe I have ever called for restructuring. I have called attention, though, to some of the tensions and some of the difficulties with the current structure. It is not for me to try and resolve those. I think, though, it is incumbent on me in my role in the industry to draw people's attention to it. I would not describe Hatfield as a Damascene conversion because these tensions have been apparent for a while. If you would like me to develop the argument, I will.'

Counsel: 'Please do.'

Corbett: 'The railway as a system, under BR it was totally integrated and one person or group of people were able to balance the system. Performance, safety, efficiency, capacity, growth, it is all one system. I think that privatization did fragment that system into over 100 different parts. That fragmentation did mean that the account-abilities were diffused and many of the different parts were set up with an economic architecture which by definition pointed them in different directions. I think it is the fragmentation and the economic incentives and the lack of clarity of accountability that actually makes it harder now to balance the system than it was then…

'I think a month ago it was unthinkable for Railtrack to contemplate bringing its maintenance in-house. We employ 12,000 people. There are around 18,000 people employed in the maintenance contractors. I think that was an unthinkable thought given the size of the management challenge. But I think now, today, after what happened at Hatfield, we have to seriously review the new form of contract that we have and whether that is going to deliver the safety and the improvements that we all require...

'Let us start with the maintenance contracts. The maintenance was outsourced on priv-atization. In 1995 the old British Rail infrastructure systems' companies were broken off. The contracts were agreed that they would maintain the railway to standards and they would get a lump sum of money to do that. That lump sum was based on what was spent on maintenance in the final years of BR and that lump was to decline by three per cent per annum over the next five years. Those were the contracts that we inherited.

'When I arrived at Railtrack at the end of 1997 the assumption was that we had a "competent contractor". No one was able to answer the question: "Which contractors are doing well, which are not?" There were no measures in place. The contractors did not have any specific targets. They had been broken off and that was the situation which we inherited...'

Counsel: 'Has adherence to performance objectives adversely affected your management of safety?'

Corbett: 'I think that answer will only be provided when we have the report on Hatfield. The tragedy at Hatfield, there was a broken rail, the rail was not in acceptable condition. I think we have to understand why speed restrictions were not put on that site. There was a number of opportunities when they could have been and they were not taken. I think when we have the answer to that we will be in a better position to be able to say whether or not the stress on performance has affected the culture at the frontline.'

Lord Cullen: 'Mr Corbett, I have some difficulty with that answer because I would have thought that if there was genuine cause for concern on this subject, that is a challenge for management to tackle the problem [promptly], if it exists?'

Corbett: 'Absolutely.'

Seven days after Corbett gave this evidence, he was sacked by his board and went on holiday to India. His replacement, Steven Marshall, also had a previous career in the financial department of Grand Metropolitan hotels. Railtrack decided that it would not bring track maintenance and renewal work in-house—the choice that Corbett called 'thinking the unthinkable'—but on November 23 it appointed its first Technical Director, Richard Middleton, and announced that it would recruit dozens of engineers (permanent way contractors had already begun to import them from India and Romania). Until then the word 'engineering' had never appeared on the floor plan of Railtrack's headquarters in London, and only rarely in the company's annual report. Middleton, a chartered civil engineer who had worked on the railways for twenty-five years, would represent engineering on the Railtrack board and report directly to the chief executive. This was a new development. Railtrack owned 10,000 route miles of track, its signalling and associated infrastructure (40,000 bridges and 750 tunnels) and yet before Hatfield it had chosen to see itself mainly as a property and contract management company, with engineering as a subdued component of the 'asset management' division. How could this be? In an interview with Nigel Harris of *Rail* magazine, Middleton said:

> We have to go back to the creation of Railtrack. Railtrack could have taken on board all of what was BR [nationalized British Rail] infrastructure, so we would have owned all the track workers, signal technicians and all overhead linesmen. But Government wanted to maximize return. It saw an opportunity by creating contracting companies that would contract with Railtrack—and they could be sold, with a revenue stream. That means you need contractual arrangements, with contracting staff overseen by a site agent and the client represented by a resident engineer—but you would have needed more engineers [in total, working for both Railtrack and its contractors] than British Rail had, it was impossible. So a unique form of contract emerged placing all engineering management—and safety responsibility—into the contracting company. Railtrack was set up as a 'light-touch' engineering resource to oversee that...But, with hindsight, it was unrealistic to expect contractors to provide network engineering resource—this is where it has all gone badly wrong.

These and other terrifying imperfections of railway privatization may have contributed to the fatal crashes at Southall in 1997 and Ladbroke Grove in 1999; Lord Cullen's verdict will be delivered when his report into the past and future of British railway safety is published later this year. But with Hatfield, the case seems beyond doubt; the crash arose from a quagmire of divided responsibility and incompetence, inspired by an ideology that placed adversarial money bargaining over human and technical cooperation, in which 'the contract' was divine. Lawyers in their legal chambers had bent their minds to the will of a government that wanted to raise as much cash as possible from the sale of public assets; and devised a scheme driven by the crudest and most unworkable notions of the free market and its competitive benefits.

By the time of the Hatfield crash, the Labour Government, elected in May 1997, had had more than three years to abolish or modify the system that was so hastily and desperately devised by its Conservative predecessor. But its actions were mainly cosmetic. OPRAF was re-designated the Strategic Rail Authority (SRA), but it remained the *shadow* Strategic Rail Authority, waiting for the Act of Parliament which would give it legal power, until

January this year. And then, despite its lengthy gestation, it turned out to be a strategic authority without a strategy. The SRA's chairman, Sir Alastair Morton, repeatedly emphasized that 'command and control' was not the authority's role. It had no specific vision of how Britain's railways should be developed; it would simply arbitrate between infrastructure schemes proposed by the private sector, subsidize those it favoured, and decide which train operating company would win which franchise. There would be no grand scheme. The SRA would not list desirable improvements to enhance a line's speed or capacity and then invite bids to meet a specification; it saw itself as a referee between rival schemes, reactive rather than pro. Its chief business would be to spend the money which had been allotted to the railways under the government's ten-year transport plan, announced in July 2000 by the Deputy Prime Minister, John Prescott, who said it would 'deliver the integrated transport system this country needs and deserves— a system fit for the new millennium and of which we can be justly proud.' Railways were to get £60bn worth of investment out of a total of £180bn—but these were 'headline' figures. In fact, only £26bn of the £60bn was guaranteed public investment, and the first figure contained about £10bn which was already committed to two large engineering projects: the upgrade of the West Coast Main Line and the new Channel Tunnel Rail Link through Kent. The other £34bn of the £60bn would come—it was hoped—from private capital, which would reap its reward from increases in railway traffic which had been projected at fifty per cent for passengers and eighty per cent for freight over the years 2001 to 2011. Return on capital would depend on this growth. After Hatfield and the slump in rail travel, such growth projections began to look fantastical. Banks and financiers in the City of London spoke of railways as a very bad bet. Railtrack began to lobby the government for increased public subsidy, arguing that otherwise the railways would remain largely unimproved.

On February 28, ten people died near Selby in Yorkshire after another Great North Eastern Railway express, this time running south from Newcastle to London at 125 mph, hit a Land-Rover and a car-carrying trailer that had somehow tumbled on to the line from an adjacent motorway only a few seconds before. The derailed express, powered by the same locomotive that had survived Hatfield, then collided with a heavy coal train travelling at 60 mph in the opposite direction. It was genuine accident, a series of unforeseeable coincidences; the way the railway was run could not be held to blame.

On March 2, one of the largest train operating companies, Sir Richard Branson's Virgin Rail, threatened to sue Railtrack unless Virgin was compensated for the £100m it had lost in revenue in passenger fares in the aftermath of Hatfield, when between October and February revenue had fallen by thirty-two per cent. Many train operating companies, including Virgin, estimated that their annual profits would be severely reduced or turned into losses. Railtrack insisted that it would not increase its total compensation to train operators from the £400m it had already announced. All over the system, shifts of workers were still renewing cracked rails. Railtrack originally estimated the cost at £100m, but others inside the railway industry suggested a more realistic estimate was £500m. The total cost of Hatfield to Railtrack could therefore be close to £1bn. Despite the likely consequences of these costs for Railtrack's profits (and some news reports mentioned bankruptcy), the company's share price remained stubbornly high. An ordinary share was worth £3.90 on flotation in 1996, peaked at £17.68 in 1998, but was still valued at £8.91 on March 6, 2001. The stock-market expectation was that the government would always bail out the company with subsidy; it could not afford to let it fail.

Government politicians said that Hatfield had created a new atmosphere within the industry, which now—at last—saw the need to 'pull together', but it is hard to find evidence to support this optimism. The world's most fragmented railway system has adversarial relationships at the heart of the philosophy which invented it, and an hour's frank conversation with most people who work in Britain's railways will eventually throw up 'mess' as their most accurate description. Animosities exist at every level: between two government departments, the Treasury and the Department of the Environment, Transport and the Regions; between two government agencies, the Rail Regulator and the Strategic Rail Authority; between a third government agency, the Health and Safety Executive, and many parts of the railway industry (the HSE was warning Railtrack about its 'weak' management of contractors as early as March 1996); between Railtrack and the train operators; and between Railtrack and its contractors.

A senior figure in the railways once told me a sad little story about the Strategic Rail Authority, then still the shadow Strategic Rail Authority. It received many foreign visitors. 'The ones from Europe come because they want to discover how *not* to privatize a railway. The ones from the Third World come to see how it might be done because the IMF has sent them. Poor mugs.'

9. Punishment

The history of large railway accidents is filled with small human mistakes; these things happen. Signalman James Tinsley, for example. Signalman Tinsley had an arrangement with his colleague, Signalman Meakin, that allowed him to start work ten minutes after his official signing-on time of 6 a.m. In that way he could reach the signal box more conveniently by the first morning train rather than rising from his bed earlier and making the two-mile walk. It was a neat arrangement for a signal box in the countryside near the Scottish border; remote from inspectors and managers, a place called Quintinshill. His colleague Meakin would work the extra ten minutes, recording the train movements during those minutes on a scrap of paper which Tinsley would then copy into the official signal box log, preserving the appearance that he had been on duty since six.

On the morning of May 22, 1915, Tinsley was preoccupied with his copying while Meakin chatted to a couple of railwaymen who had come into the box. The First World War was nine months old. The line Meakin and Tinsley controlled was the main route from England to Scotland, busy with trains of troops and naval coal. A northbound local—the train that Tinsley had arrived on—had been shunted by Meakin on to the southbound line to allow a late-running night express from London to overtake it. There it lay outside the box, forgotten. At 6.42, the next signal box to the north indicated to Tinsley that a special train was on its way south. Would Quintinshill accept it? Tinsley set the signals to green. At 6.48, the special came down the gradient at high speed carrying troops of the Royal Scots Regiment bound for Liverpool and the Dardanelles. The special hit the local, and then, coming in the opposite direction and also at speed, the night express ran into the wreckage of both. All the carriages were wooden and those of the troop train lit by gas. A great fire burned at Quintinshill for twenty-four hours. Of the 227 dead, all but ten were young men of the Royal Scots.

A Scottish court found Tinsley and Meakin guilty of culpable homicide. Tinsley was sentenced to three years in jail and Meakin to eighteen months, but they were pardoned within a year. Both men had suffered severe nervous breakdowns.

The politicians and their advisers who, in Corbett's phrase, 'ripped apart' Britain's railways have never spoken publicly about the crash at Howe Dell, though sometimes their successors in the Conservative Party have admitted that 'they got some things wrong'. They have directorships, they sit on boards, they have lunch at the club. So far as we know, they sleep soundly at night. A nervous breakdown or two would be just.

Significant numbers

Public subsidy via Treasury grants to Britain's railways in
their last year of public ownership, 1993–94:   £1.073bn
Public subsidy via the shadow Strategic Rail Authority to
Britain's private train operating companies, 1999–2000:

£1.348bn

Amount that lawyers were paid per working day on the
Conservative Government's railway privatization programme,
1992–97:   £23,000
Growth in the number of Britain's lawyers, 1975–2000:

400 per cent

Decline in number of applications to study civil engineering at
British universities, 1994–99:   40 per cent
Members of the House of Commons who have qualified as
civil, chemical, electrical, mechanical or marine engineers:

7 out of 659

Members of the House of Commons who have trained in civil,
commercial or criminal law: 70 out of 659
Salary and benefits paid to Gerald Corbett in his last year as
Railtrack's chief executive: £398,000
Pay-off to Gerald Corbett from Railtrack: 'A six-figure sum'
Estimate of salary and benefits that Gerald Corbett will receive
for six months' work in his new job as executive chairman of
the Woolworth shopping chain (appointed February 28, 2001):

£500,000

Where are they now?

Paul Channon, now Baron Kelvedon, of Ongar in the County of Essex. *Then*: Secretary of State for Transport, 1987–89, and advocate of railway privatization. *Now*: president, the Old Etonian Association.

Cecil Parkinson, now Baron Parkinson, of Carnforth in the County of Lancashire. *Then*: Secretary of State for Transport, 1989–90, and advocate of railway privatization. *Now*: a director of Resolution Security Ltd, Integrated Technology (Europe) Ltd, The Wordsworth Trust, McNicholas plc, Vdata Ltd, Holf Technologies Ltd, Huntswood CTC Ltd, Huntswood plc, Energis Squared Ltd, Mobile Phone Supercover Ltd, Odysey Corporation plc, Amertrans Ltd. Lord Parkinson's residence is an old vicarage in Hertfordshire, a few miles from the site of the Hatfield crash.

Malcolm Rifkind, now Sir Malcolm Rifkind, KCMG, PC, QC. *Then*: Secretary of State for Transport, 1990–92, and early planner of railway privatization. *Now*: president of the Scottish Conservatives; director of Ramco Energy plc, Foreign & Colonial Markets Investment Trust, British Assets Investment Trust, Authoriszor Inc; consultant to BHP petroleum, Price Waterhouse Coopers, Petrofac UK Ltd.

John MacGregor, OBE, PC. *Then*: Secretary of State for Transport, 1992–94, and implementer of railway privatization. *Now*: Conservative MP for South Norfolk; director of Associated British Foods plc, Slough Estates plc, Uniq plc,

IAN JACK

Friends Provident, the Supervisory Board of DAF Trucks N.V.
Dr Brian Mawhinney, now Sir Brian Mawhinney, knight, PC.
Then: Secretary of State for Transport, 1994–95, and
implementer of railway privatization. *Now*: Conservative MP
for Cambridgeshire North-West; director, Andras House Ltd,
Stiell Ltd, WR2 (Indianapolis).

Sir George Young, sixth baronet, PC. *Then*: Secretary of State
for Transport, 1995–97, and implementer of railway
privatization. *Now*: Conservative MP for NW Hampshire;
director, McCarthy and Stone plc. Recreation: bicycling.

John Major, CH, PC. *Then*: Prime Minister and First Lord of
the Treasury, 1990–97, and advocate and implementer of
railway privatization. *Now*: Conservative MP for Huntingdon;
president of Surrey County Cricket Club, member of the
Carlton Club and the MCC; remunerated director, The
Mayflower Corporation plc; remunerated member, the
European Advisory Board of the Carlyle Group (Washington),
the European Advisory Board of the Emerson Electric
Company (St Louis); remunerated speaker to audiences in the
United Kingdom and, via the Washington Speakers Bureau,
abroad. Between February 1999 and January 2000, he visited
the United States six times on speaking tours and also delivered
paid speeches to business audiences in Kuwait, Bermuda,
Spain, Geneva, Strasbourg and Saudi Arabia.

When not abroad, he continues to live forty miles up the East
Coast Main Line from Hatfield, at Huntingdon.

Acknowledgments

Documents

The Health and Safety Executive's first and second interim reports into the Hatfield crash; reports of the House of Commons Select Committee on Transport; Railtrack's annual report and accounts for 1999–2000; the shadow Strategic Rail Authority's annual report 1999–2000; press notices issued by the Office of the Rail Regulator, the Health and Safety Executive, and the Department of the Environment, Transport and the Regions; *Rail Failure Assessment* by Transportation Technology Center, Inc., Pueblo, Colorado; transcripts of proceedings of the Ladbroke Grove Rail Inquiry, Part 2, chaired by Lord Cullen, PC; the House of Commons Register of Members' Interests.

Books

Biddle and Simmons (ed.), *The Oxford Companion to British Railway History*, Oxford 1997

Freeman and Shaw (ed.), *All Change: British Railway Privatisation*, London 2000

Grinling, Charles H., *The History of the Great Northern Railway*, 1898, rev. edn. London 1966

The Institution of Civil Engineers, *Modern Railway Transportation*, 1993

Jack, Harry, *Locomotives of the London and North-Western Railway Southern Divison*, 2001

Lee, Charles E., *The Evolution of Permanent Way*, 1937
Lee, Charles E., *The Evolution of Railways*, 1937
Lewis, M. J. T., *Early Wooden Railways,* 1970
MacDermot, E. T., *History of the Great Western Railway*, London 1927, rev. by C. R. Clinker, 1964
Mase, Armin and Schneider, Ascanio, *Railway Accidents of Great Britain and Europe*, Zurich 1968, London 1970
Nock, O. S., *Historic Railway Disasters*, London 1966
Rolt, L. T. C., *Red For Danger*, London 1976
British Railway Track Design, Construction and Maintenance: A Handbook of the Permanent Way Institution, 1993

Magazines

Rail, Modern Railways (particularly pieces by Roger Ford), *The Railway Magazine*

Websites

The Health and Safety Executive: www.hse.gov.uk
Railtrack: www.railtrack.co.uk
Ladbroke Grove (The Cullen Inquiry): www.lgri.org.uk
The Office of the Rail Regulator: www.rail-reg.gov.uk

I am also grateful to Bill Armstrong of the Permanent Way Institution, Jonathan Bray of Transport 2000, and the librarians of the Institutions of both Civil and Mechanical Engineers; finally to the research and knowledge of Fatema Ahmed, John Ware and Christian Wolmar.

Read on...

This book is an expanded version of a piece published in the Spring 2001 issue of *Granta* magazine—*Granta* 73: *Necessary Journeys*.

If you would like to continue to read good writing about things that matter, why not subscribe to *Granta*? Since 1979, *Granta* has published many of the world's finest writers tackling some of the world's most important subjects, from intimate human experiences to the large public and political events that have shaped all our lives. *Granta* is published quarterly, as a handsome paperback of at least 256 pages. Subscribers get *Granta* delivered to their homes, at a substantial discount.

'In its blend of memoirs, photojournalism and reportage, and in its championing of contemporary realist fiction, Granta has its face pressed firmly against the window, determined to witness the world.'   *Observer*

Find out more at:
www.granta.com/readon
Granta, 2/3 Hanover Yard,
Noel Road, London N1 8BE
Tel 020 7704 0470

GRANTA
THE MAGAZINE OF NEW WRITING